...ELEGANCE IS A STATE OF MIND.

Oleg Cassini

Fashion is not something that exists in dresses only.
Fashion is in the sky, in the street,
fashion has to do with ideas, the way we live,
what is happening.

COCO CHANEL

WHEN
IN DOUBT,
WEAR RED.

Bill Blass

I THINK
THERE IS BEAUTY
IN EVERYTHING.

Alexander McQueen

Don't be into trends.
Don't make fashion own you,
but you decide what you are,
what you want to express
by the way you dress
and the way you live.

GIANNI VERSACE

Style is a way to say
who you are without
having to speak.

RACHEL ZOE

...I have learned
that what is
important in a dress
is the woman
who is wearing it.

YVES SAINT LAURENT

Oh, never mind the fashion.
When one has a style of one's own,
it is always twenty times better.

MARGARET OLIPHANT